GINGERBREAD GEMS
OF WILLIMANTIC, CONNECTICUT

Michele Palmer

Photography by Lori Garris

4880 Lower Valley Road, Atglen, PA 19310 USA

A Note About the Name

Willimantic is a district in the town of Windham, Connecticut, which also includes South Windham, North Windham, and Windham Center. Except for the chapter on the Windhams, and unless otherwise noted, all the photos were taken in Willimantic.

Other Schiffer Books by Michele Palmer
Toile: The Storied Fabrics of Europe and America

Other Schiffer Books on Related Subjects
Gingerbread Gems of Ocean Grove, New Jersey, by Tina Skinner
Gingerbread Gems: Victorian Architecture of Cape May, by Tina Skinner & Bruce Waters

Photographs © Lori Garris
Copyright © 2007 by Michele Palmer
Library of Congress Control Number: 2006934289

Designed by Mark David Bowyer
Type set in DeRoos / Arrus BT

ISBN: 0-7643-2603-1
Printed in China

Published by Schiffer Publishing Ltd.
4880 Lower Valley Road
Atglen, PA 19310
Phone: (610) 593-1777; Fax: (610) 593-2002
E-mail: Info@schifferbooks.com

For the largest selection of fine reference books on this and related subjects, please visit our web site at
www.schifferbooks.com
We are always looking for people to write books on new and related subjects. If you have an idea for a book please contact us at the above address.

This book may be purchased from the publisher.
Include $3.95 for shipping.
Please try your bookstore first.
You may write for a free catalog.

In Europe, Schiffer books are distributed by
Bushwood Books
6 Marksbury Ave.
Kew Gardens
Surrey TW9 4JF England
Phone: 44 (0) 20 8392-8585; Fax: 44 (0) 20 8392-9876
E-mail: info@bushwoodbooks.co.uk
Website: www.bushwoodbooks.co.uk
Free postage in the U.K., Europe; air mail at cost.

CONTENTS

ACKNOWLEDGMENTS

This book, like much of the revival of Victorian Willimantic, was a community effort. Foremost among those who helped in its creation were Beverly York, Educational Consultant at the Windham Textile & History Museum, and Robert and Pam Horrocks, leaders of the Willimantic Victorian Neighborhood Association. Other helpful folk included local historian Thomas Beardsley, and Ron Lincoln, Shirley Slye, Penny Tracy, and others at the Willimantic Camp Meeting Association. Our gratitude also extends to all the homeowners, neighbors, and others we met during our photo shoots, who offered their cooperation and, sometimes, food and drink. Tina Skinner, Donna Baker, and the staff at Schiffer Books provided excellent advice and assistance. Finally, our deep thanks go to our families, who supported us at every step along the way.

INTRODUCTION

During the late nineteenth century—the height of the Victorian Age—Willimantic, Connecticut was one of the most prosperous cities in New England. Its name means "land of the swift running water" in Algonquin, and, indeed, it was the rushing waters of the Willimantic River that provided power to run the textile mills, which were the source of the city's prosperity. Also contributing to the success of the mills was the city's status as a major railroad hub for New England, with fifty trains a day passing through town.

The largest mill in the city, the Willimantic Linen Company, known after 1898 as the American Thread Company, was the world's leading manufacturer of thread, earning Willimantic the nickname of "Thread City." Besides being internationally recognized for the quantity—and quality—of its product, the company was a role model for the treatment of its workers, and for the aesthetics and innovation of its architecture.

One of the Willimantic Linen Company's buildings was the largest industrial building in the world when it was constructed in 1884, and was the first new factory to be wired for electricity, with a system designed by Thomas Edison. Its interior was filled with paintings on paneled walls, and stained glass windows that ran the entire length of the immense structure, presumably to create a pleasant working environment as well as to show off the company's phenomenal success. A charming Queen Anne building that now houses the Windham Textile & History Museum was once the company store and free library, where evening classes in art, singing, and literacy were offered. Skilled laborers were able to rent company-owned single family dwellings in a choice of several styles (although unskilled workers still lived in boarding houses or multi-family row houses).

Of course, idealizing whatever amenities this huge industrial complex offered can obscure the harsher realities of mill life. Whether for good or bad, there is no doubt that the mill had profound effects, not only on its workers, but on the community at large.

Between 1870 and 1890, as industry expanded, the city's population doubled, and so did the need for housing. While workers' dwellings clustered around the mill site, middle and upper class homes were concentrated elsewhere. The mill's top management, bankers, and railroad officials created impressive mansions across the river along Windham

Windham Mills, Main Street. The Willimantic Linen Company, later known as the American Thread Company, built this granite structure in 1864 as part of its expanding mill complex. The granite came from the Willimantic River behind it, which also provided power for the mills before the advent of electricity. The building is currently being developed into residential, retail, and commercial space.

Road. Other well-to-do families built equally grand homes in South Windham and Windham Center, rural villages just outside the city limits. The large and affluent middle class of merchants, professionals, and skilled artisans developed the city's most extensive Victorian neighborhood, known as Prospect Hill. Another enclave of Victorian architecture, the Willimantic Camp Meeting Association, was a summer religious retreat established in 1860, with tiny gingerbread cottages that now provide year-round residences.

All told, Willimantic has the most Victorian homes per capita on the East Coast, and is second only to San Francisco in privately owned Victorian homes.

When the American Thread Company began moving some of its operations south in the decades after World War II, the prominence of the city began to decline. Its status as a railroad center also plummeted, as cars and trucks replaced passenger and freight trains. Main Street businesses—whose buildings are fine examples of Victorian architecture as well—were hurt by urban renewal projects and suburban shopping malls. The final blow came in 1985, when the American Thread Company closed its doors completely, and left the city in an economic crisis. Some of the grandest Victorian structures fell into disrepair, while others were covered in vinyl siding and divided into multi-family or student housing.

In the last fifteen years, however, a remarkable revival began taking place, based largely on the city's Victorian heritage. The mill buildings are being redeveloped into housing, retail and commercial space, as well as artists' studios and galleries. The Windham Textile & History Museum is preserving the history of the area's textile industry, and the Connecticut Eastern Railroad Museum is doing the same for its railroad history. The river is being reclaimed, with an annual Riverfest and proposed whitewater and riverside parks. Popular celebrations include the Fourth of July Boom Box Parade and the Third Thursday Street Festival, both held on Main Street, which is now on the National Register of Historic Places, as is Windham Center and Prospect Hill.

Most important of all, however, is the steady, one-by-one restoration of many of the Victorian houses throughout the city. Leading the restoration movement is the Willimantic Victorian Neighborhood Association, with its annual Victorian Home Tour held during the first weekend in June. The city is once again blossoming, with Victorian architecture as the centerpiece of its renaissance. It may no longer be "Thread City," but it is definitely earning its new nickname: "Romantic Willimantic."

Windham Textile & History Museum, Main Street.
The Queen Anne building that houses the museum once served as the thread company's store and workers' library. In fulfilling its mission to preserve the history of the textile industry in Connecticut, the museum features period settings, including this Victorian dining room from a mill manager's home.

Windham Town Hall, Main Street
The clock tower of the 1896 town hall makes it one of the tallest buildings on Main Street. The building to the right, once the post office, is now the Willimantic Brewing Company and Main Street Café, a popular pub and restaurant.

Willimantic Victorian Neighborhood Association, Main Street.
This grass roots organization sponsors activities from small neighborhood garden parties to its major annual event—the Victorian Home Tour, held the first weekend in June.

A horse-drawn wagon on Prospect Street transports visitors during the annual Victorian Home Tour.

Thread City Crossing,
Main & Jackson Streets.
This town landmark, built in 2000
and known familiarly as the Frog
Bridge, spans the Willimantic River.
Its twelve foot high bronze frogs created by sculptor Leo Jensen and the
concrete spools they sit on combine a
local legend about frogs with a symbol
of the town's foremost former industry—thread manufacturing.

Eugene Boss House, 100 Windham Road, c. 1880s.
The seventeen-room Stick style home is painted pale celery with tansy green trim. At
the time of the photograph, the trim and red accent colors hadn't been completed.

CHAPTER 1
MANSIONS AND MORE: WINDHAM ROAD

Across the river from the mill complex are the former residences of some of its top management. These bosses (including one whose last name actually was "Boss") lived close enough to walk over a small bridge to work, though their houses remained separated by river and trees from the hectic activity of the mill.

Bankers, railroad officials, and other businessmen also found the area to be a desirable location. Within a short stretch of the road, examples of most of the major architectural styles of the Victorian period are represented, including Queen Anne, Stick, Italianate, and Carpenter Gothic.

Eugene Boss House, 100 Windham Road, c. 1880s.
Boss was the longtime manager of the Willimantic Linen Company, and could literally oversee the mill from his home.

A view of the side porch reveals the textile mill's smokestack in the background.

James Reid House, 88 Windham Road, c. 1884.
Another Stick style but with elements of Romanesque Revival in its stone first floor and entry. Reid was the textile mill's chief chemist, who developed color-fast dyes.

The recessed entry features a rounded arch and a short, squat colonnette typical of the Romanesque style. It is complemented by a mosaic exterior entrance floor.

Detail of the mosaic exterior entrance floor.

Judge John Manning Hall House, 125 Windham Road, c. 1883.
This stately brick and shingle Queen Anne was built by a prominent citizen who later became president of the New York, New Haven, and Hartford Railroad. The magnificent copper beech trees in front were planted at the time the house was built.

A feature of Queen Anne homes is the variety in size, shape, and treatment of the windows.

George Stiles House, 103 Windham Road, c. 1875. The main section of this brick home is in the Italianate style, with painted bricks in place of wood molding over the windows. An octagonal tower and porch were added later, probably after 1905.

Round Tuscan columns on the carousel porch are echoed in smaller versions on the second floor side porch.

Marshal Tilden House, 113 Windham Road, c. 1880
Maroon trim makes a pleasing contrast to the light olive clapboard siding of this Stick style home.

Dwight Potter House, 76 Windham Road, c. 1875.
Although greatly modified in the twentieth century, this Stick style house still retains its decorative
cross-bracing in the gables and iron finials on top of the tower.

89 Windham Road, c. 1900.
A carousel porch balanced by a portico on the opposite side adds interest to this otherwise simple Victorian house.

The portico frames
a double front door.

Charles Utley House, 77 Windham Road, c. 1880.
Gargoyles guard the front steps of this Carpenter Gothic painted in confectionary shades of pink, purple, yellow, and green.

The patterned slate roof adds an extra "gingerbread-house" touch to this charming cottage.

71 Windham Road, 1870.
Another modest Victorian era house with some Italianate features is distinguished by a rickrack frieze on
the porch cornice and a teal, maroon, and cream color scheme.

CHAPTER 2
FANCY HOMES, SIMPLE VILLAGES: THE WINDHAMS

Just outside the city limits, these "suburbs" are actually rural villages, typical of New England, each with its own library, post office, and cluster of historic homes, many of which date back to colonial times. Windham Center, which is on the National Register of Historic Places, is predominantly an agricultural village, while South Windham is an industrial village built around several small factories. The Victorian entrepreneurs who built homes here added to the status of both communities.

4 Main Street, South Windham, 1872.
This classic white Italianate is graced with a wide verandah, front gables, and a cupola with quadruple double-hung windows on each side.

***Guilford Smith House, 9 Main
Street, South Windham, 1877.***
Brown shingles contrast with
white woodwork and white
dogwoods in this rambling
Queen Anne.

Timbering in the gables
adds Stick style details.

Four rocking chairs on the front porch of the house below seem to be waiting for visitors.

Harvey Winchester House, 11 Main Street, South Windham, 1890.
Flowering dogwoods nearly obscure the front of this Shingle style home and its gambrel roofline. The original owner and his next-door neighbor, Charles Smith, owned a factory down the street, which produced a paper drying and cutting machine that revolutionized the production of paper. Charles' son, Guilford, lived on the other side of the Winchester house until he moved to Windham Center (see following pages).

Miss Laura Huntington House, 10 Windham Center Road, Windham Center, c. 1850
This stately Italianate home is made lively by a coat of bubblegum-pink paint with contrasting black and white trim.

Hood molding and ornate brackets
are the main decorative features.

Guilford Smith House, 3 Plains Road, Windham Center, 1885. Two views of this sunny yellow Italianate home show the fencing that surrounds the property and echoes the porch balustrade.

The white trim and bracketing in the home are picked out in dark green to match the shutters.

Baker-Weir House, 29 Windham Center Road, Windham Center, 1750/1860.
Two Italianate wings were added to the original colonial farmhouse, as was the fanciful arcaded porch. The American impressionist, J. Alden Weir, spent summers here and painted scenes of the textile mills and other local landscapes. He died in 1919 and is buried in the Windham Center Cemetery.

Light shines through the pierced patterns onto the door's sidelight. The porch was undergoing renovations at the time of the photograph.

Baker-Weir
House
1750/1860

CHAPTER 3
THE JEWEL IN THE CROWN: PROSPECT HILL

Within a forty-block area north of Main Street lies the city's largest concentration of Victorian homes. This area comprises over eight hundred houses, along with schools, churches, and a fire station, most of which were built between 1865 and 1910. All major styles of the Victorian period are represented, as well as examples of the later Craftsman style. The entire Prospect Hill district is on the National Register of Historic Places, making it one of the largest historic districts in Connecticut. Rising steeply from its southern boundary to a four hundred foot summit, the Hill afforded remarkable prospects, or views of the city and surrounding countryside. Here, the growing middle class of the late nineteenth and early twentieth centuries, many with offices or businesses on Main Street, built homes and raised families. It remains a quiet, tree-lined, residential neighborhood.

Edwin Bugbee House, 97 Prospect Street, c. 1875.
The gold and green tile design in the mansard roof is the crowning touch of this Second Empire home. Those colors are picked out in some of the trim details.

The current owner of the Edwin Bugbee house added a new fountain and surrounding stonework, which matches a sidewalk retaining wall.

A stonework fountain was built on the side of the house.

Captain Stephen Morse House, 116 Prospect Street, c. 1875.
Ornate crowns on the dormer windows, striped awnings, and a crisp cream, tan, and brown color scheme add up to a ship-shape Second Empire fit for a sea captain.

William Grant House, 291 Prospect Street, 1895.
Although there are Stick elements here, the basic style is Queen Anne, with its steep, cross-gabled roof, wraparound porch, and prominent tower. The property is owned by Eastern Connecticut State University and used for university special events.

Arthur Carpenter House, 156 Prospect Street, 1889.
Vibrant blue shingles and a witch-hat tower distinguish this Queen Anne.

George Tiffany House, 272 Prospect Street, c. 1890.
The carousel porch was popular on Queen Anne houses, perhaps as a reminder of a favorite Victorian amusement for children.

Frank Larabee House, 55 Prospect Street, 1891.
The welcoming corner entry of this Queen Anne shows off its gables, tower, and carousel porch.

A side view of the house.

Hyde Kingsley House, 133 Prospect Street, 1883.
At the corner of Church and Prospect is the House of Eight Gables, although
only a few are visible from this view. The most dramatic feature of the house is
the elaborately carved chimney with its stained glass window.

Details of the chimney.

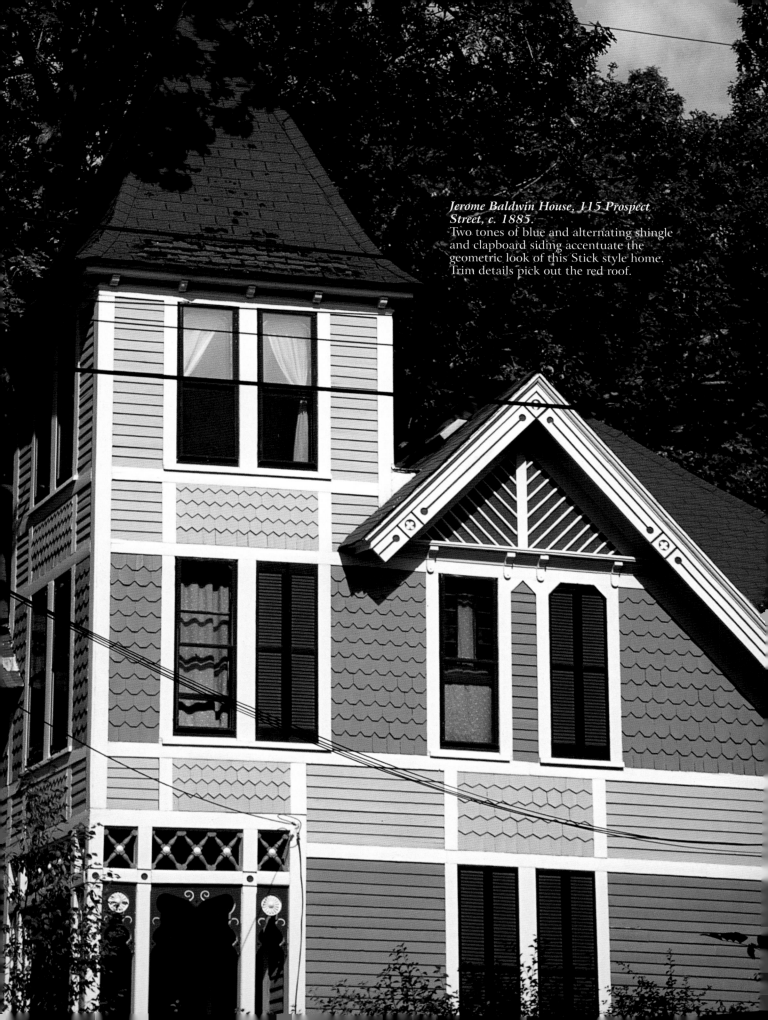

Jerome Baldwin House, 115 Prospect Street, c. 1885.
Two tones of blue and alternating shingle and clapboard siding accentuate the geometric look of this Stick style home. Trim details pick out the red roof.

Arthur Bill House, 183 Prospect Street, c. 1887.
This unusual house fore-shadows the boxy Four Square design that was popular in the early twentieth century, even as it incorporates Queen Anne and Shingle style features.

The main exterior ornamentations are the sunburst designs, swags, and compass-look gable design.

Burt Thompson House, 275 Prospect Street, 1896.
The Italianate double-decker porch is adorned with various
Eastlake designs on its posts and balustrades.

*Joseph Riordan House, 305
Prospect Street, c. 1890*
A wraparound verandah
with top and bottom bal-
ustrades graces this creamy
vernacular Victorian.

Giles Alford House, 200 Prospect Street, 1880.
Carpenter Gothic ornamentation and a flower-filled porch
adorn this otherwise simple house.

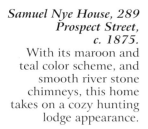

*Samuel Nye House, 289
Prospect Street,
c. 1875.*
With its maroon and
teal color scheme, and
smooth river stone
chimneys, this home
takes on a cozy hunting
lodge appearance.

Frank Webb House, 214 Church Street, 1882.
This multi-gabled Queen Anne was built by a banker and
director of the Windham Silk Company who made his fortune
in the retail clothing trade.

The red roof and earth tone paint
scheme were chosen to complement a
huge copper beech tree on the property,
once the largest in New England before
it had to be cut down in 2005.

John McDonald House, 215 Church Street, c. 1890.
Until recently, this home had been in a family of newspaper editors and publishers for five generations. The brick porch and second floor tower were added in 1903. Around the same time, the dining room was remodeled by Gustav Stickley, founder of the American Arts and Crafts movement, whose oak paneling, ceiling beams, sconces and lamps still remain.

George Taylor House,
193 Church Street,
c. 1890.
Pastel colors and a different sunrise motif in each gable adds distinction to this combination Queen Anne/Stick style home.

Dr. John Bentley House, 180 Church Street, c. 1890
Green, yellow, and coral colors impart a whimsical flavor to this Queen Anne with its octagonal tower.

Frank Wilson House, 196 Church Street, c. 1891.
Architect C.T. Beardsley designed this dignified Queen Anne using cypress wood, plate glass windows, and swag friezes in the bays.

Origen Hall House, 147 Church Street, c. 1865.
All the signature features of an Italianate house are here, including the tower, front porch, side bay, bracketing in the eaves and a triple, round-arched window in the gable.

J. Deloraine Conant House, 71 Chestnut Street, c. 1890.
The pastel yellow clapboard is punc-tuated with red window casing and alternating blue striped shingles in the gables.

Charles Leonard House, 78 Walnut Street, 1886.
This small Queen Anne with Stick style elements sports a witch-hat tower.

84 Walnut Street, 1887.
A sister house to number
78, the Stick style boards
here are more prominent.
Note the similarities in
the gable details.

Samuel Harvey House, 281 Walnut Street, c. 1878.
Hooded windows in the Carpenter Gothic style add interest to this Victorian.

Right:
John Lewis House, 317 Jackson Street, 1862.
Situated next to a small park—the site of poetry readings in the summer months—this Italianate home is one of the earliest examples of that style in the city.

Simple bracketing in the eaves and simple molding around the windows create an understated but elegant look.

John Hennessey House, 190 Jackson Street, c. 1890.
The pale pink, raspberry and white color scheme is punctuated by gold leaf details on the posts, brackets, and metal fencing.

John Hickey House, 226-228 Jackson Street, c. 1890.
This symmetrical duplex is unified by a center gable with striking red scrollwork.

Mary Clark House, 74 Windham Street, 1896. Bright spring flowers contrast with the subdued colors of this Queen Anne. Note the spiral-turned porch posts.

Right:
Rev. Edward George House, 90 Windham Street, 1896. This home exhibits a more pronounced Shingle style, with the curved recess around the gable windows and the shortened tower.

The flared bottom of the gable adds a Shingle style element to the side of the house.

Albert Turner House, 98 Windham Street, 1894. Porthole windows, iron cresting, and wavy diagonal boards in the tower impart a nautical flavor to this Queen Anne, reminiscent of a seaside residence.

Albert Scripture House, 114 Windham Street, 1895. Shades of teal and terra cotta complement each other in this crisp Queen Anne.

Wilton Little House, 122 Windham Street, c. 1896.
Decorative carving in the gables and a swag frieze are the icing on this pink Queen Anne confection.
The shingled porch skirt and rounded balcony are Shingle style elements.

John Tracy House, 125 Summit Street, c. 1893.
This gold Queen Anne set high on a hill also features a Shingle style verandah and second floor porch.

Joseph Dwight Chaffee House, 183 Summit Street, c. 1889.
The property on which Colonel Chaffee built his home was considered the most desirable lot in Willimantic. It is set off by a cobblestone retaining wall topped by an evergreen hedge.

A side view of the house shows part of its extensive wraparound porch and the "C" for "Chaffee" in the weathervane.

A detail of the portico gable and simple stained glass window above it.

Edwin Buck House, 150 North Street, 1876.
This Second Empire house features ornate hood molding in the dormer windows.

Fred Jordan House, 190 North Street, c. 1890.
A five color paint scheme in shades of blue, taupe, dusty rose, brown and terra cotta accentuates this Queen Anne's multi-gables and large wraparound porch.

William Jordan House, 228 North Street, c. 1895.
A brother and business partner of Fred Jordan, who lived at 190 North Street, William built this somewhat more modest Queen Anne. Besides a two story bay, it sports multi-paned specialty windows in its front façade.

Thomas Jefferson Little House, 232 North Street, c. 1888.
In frothy shades of cream, coral, pink, and rose, with dark green details, this Victorian vernacular incorporates Eastlake decoration in its front porch.

A bay window and side porch on the house at left look over a recently landscaped garden, which the owner calls a "new Victorian secret garden."

168 Summit Street, c. 1890.
Not all the homes on Prospect Hill were built by the upper middle class. Some of the most charming ones are small Victorian cottages such as this one.

The garden is built around a giant maple tree.

A side view of the house reveals its depth, along with pretty bay windows and shutters.

Edgar Young House, 255 High Street, c. 1888.
This pristine Victorian cottage is painted in shades of blue, lavender, taupe, and white.

The opposite side view taken in spring shows off a flowering rhododendron and antique water pump.

The iron lantern hanging from a pillar at the Albert Morse house is one of dozens of candles, torches, lanterns, and kerosene lamps that are lit during the owners' annual "Lighting of the Garden" party.

A clock in the garden may not be a typical Victorian accessory, but it is ornamental and useful.

Albert Morse House, 202 Lewiston Avenue, c. 1890.
This charming Queen Anne cottage is painted in a vibrant gold and plum color scheme with cream and green accents.

Frank Bugbee House, 76 Bellevue Street, c. 1901. Curved, multi-paned windows, a rhododendron in full bloom and two dogs in the driveway add to the charm of this late Victorian home with Shingle style influences.

CHAPTER 4
A GINGERBREAD RETREAT: WILLIMANTIC CAMP MEETING ASSOCIATION

Like other camp meeting grounds across the country, this Methodist summer retreat offered prayer meetings, sermons, and singing in an idyllic outdoor setting. The retreat proved so popular that a special railroad station was built near the site to accommodate the crowds. Most of the buildings date from 1868 to 1877. Of the three hundred original cottages, only one hundred are still standing, many destroyed by the 1938 hurricane. Retreats and Sunday services are still held during the summer.

Wesley Circle
A trio of cottages nestle among the trees.

Left:
Barrows Cottage, 18 Church Circle, 1868.
The Barrows Cottage is one of the earliest buildings in the camp ground. Its board-and-batten siding, gable bracing, and large rounded window are typical elements of the Carpenter Gothic style, as are the pendants that hang like icicles from the eaves.

Church Circle
Three of the original public buildings are still in use today (left to right): the Children's Building, the Library, and the Ladies Improvement Society.

35 Haven Avenue
Orange and white friezes below the porch cornice and railings contribute to the cheerful look of this cottage.

57 Haven Avenue
Shocking pink decorative elements brighten this otherwise plain gray shingled cottage.

JUST-A-MERE
COTTAGE

92

92 Wesley Circle
"Just-A-Mere Cottage" says it all of this blue
Carpenter Gothic gingerbread house.

Moorish keyhole designs create a dramatic entranceway and extend throughout the porch.

CHAPTER 5
PORCHES AND PORTICOS

More than links between the outdoors and the indoors, porches and porticos in the Victorian era were style statements in their own right. From tiny service porches to grand, wraparound verandahs, all were opportunities for both architectural and floral decoration.

Planters overflow with blooms atop a simple railing and slat balustrade.

Hanging and potted plants make a pink and yellow porch even more cheerful.

Abacus-like spindles add
interest to this inviting
wraparound porch.

Another graceful wraparound porch.

A variety of spindles, brackets, and pierced designs enliven this pretty front porch.

Gold-leaf decorations in the posts and arches add elegance to a simple side porch.

Gold-leaf is painted more prominently on these posts.

This small side porch features a variety of quatrefoils, or clover designs, as well as a roped faux post on the bottom of the real post.

Double posts and brackets distinguish this carousel porch.

Flags and flowers enhance
this small portico.

This side view of a portico
presents four levels of interesting
designs, including the negative
spaces created by the balusters.

This portico makes a grand entrance even without an attached front porch.

Simple posts massed together add up to an impressive statement.

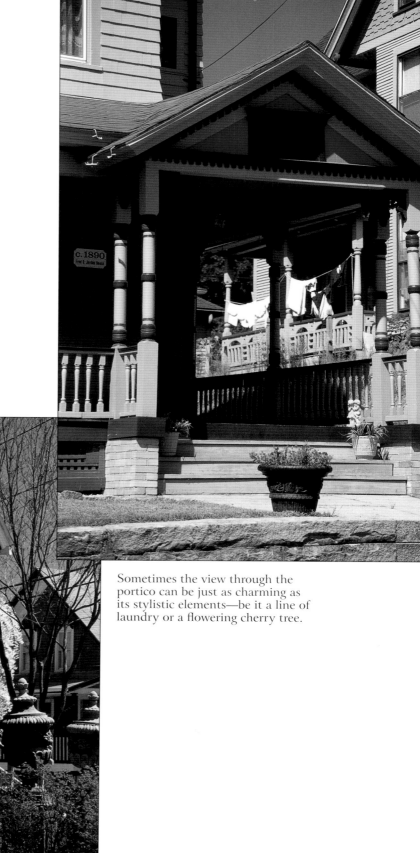

Sometimes the view through the
portico can be just as charming as
its stylistic elements—be it a line of
laundry or a flowering cherry tree.

Right:
A quartet of porticos features a
variety of scrollwork, shingles
and spindles.

A plain brown door is paired with a stained glass window in a simple, but striking arrangement.

CHAPTER 6
DOORS AND WINDOWS

Among the most expressive features of a Victorian home are its doors and windows. Stained glass, in particular, is found in abundance, and even small Victorian vernacular homes often boast a stained glass window or two.

Small gabled roofs supported by brackets provide rain protection and visual interest above these doorways.

Carved red double doors look beautiful framed in soft gold.

The three doorways of Thread City Café, a Main Street restaurant, are echoed in the triple window bays on the second and third floors.

Two-story bays were also found on Italianate style residences, as well as commercial buildings.

The rope trim on this bay is painted gold, which creates the effect of real braiding and matches the nearby maple tree's fall foliage. A small balcony above is the crowning touch.

Lacy gingerbread dangles like jewelry over these bay windows.

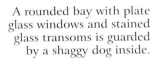

A rounded bay with plate glass windows and stained glass transoms is guarded by a shaggy dog inside.

A single arch-head window is surrounded by panes of stained glass.

The arch of this window is created by its fanciful molding. At one time, the window itself was probably arched as well.

Above the simple round arch windows are ornately carved brackets accented with pink pendants and rope trim under the eaves.

A Palladian window, recently restored by the owner, is a typical feature of a Shingle style home, as is the gambrel roofline.

Double pointed-head Gothic windows are framed by shutters in pastel colors.

Six original fleur-de-lis stained glass panels surround a more recent center window addition.

A single recessed corner window is enhanced by an intricately carved planter.

Double corner windows are set off by small, decorative balconies.

The molding above the dormer window picks up the floral motif in the tile mansard roof.

This dormer serves as the peak of the entire house.

The conical roof of this dormer ends
in a spiral wire that may once have
been the base for a weathervane.

CHAPTER 7

TOWERS AND GABLES

Reaching to the heights, along with the aspirations of their homeowners, these peaks create the distinctive skyline of Willimantic.

Four-sided towers are typical of Italianate houses. Note the distinctive cutaway corner at the lower left.

This short squat tower, one step beyond a dormer window, is a common element of Shingle style houses.

Left:
The witch-hat tower and compass-look gable design complement each other.

An octagonal tower is more unusual for an Italianate house and may have been added later.

Stick style trim, a four-color paint scheme, and other decorative elements adorn this standout tower.

The top of this octagonal tower creates a lookout from every angle.

Although the timbering in this Stick style tower hadn't been picked out yet at the time of the photograph, the sheer variety of shingles and boards add interest and texture.

Right:
This square tower is
set at a jaunty angle to
the rest of the house.

An original 1890's weathervane sits at the top of a barn tower in South Windham.

The onion dome tower roof is echoed in the rounded windows and arcaded second floor porch.

Stars and stripes distinguish this gable bracing.

Simple bracing in the side gable becomes slightly more elaborate in the front gable.

Fanciful scrollwork adds a decorative touch to these bracings.

While the red scrollwork looks purely decorative, it also adds support to the gable.

Pierced bargeboards come in two sizes in these Stick style gables.

94

Two other Stick style gables.

Pastel colors add a light touch to the scrollwork that completely fills the gable.

CHAPTER 8
A SEASONAL SCRAPBOOK

Each season sets off Willimantic's Victorian architecture in a distinct way. Spring pastels soften the edges of angular forms. Summer blossoms add color to monochromatic paint schemes. Blazing fall foliage creates dramatic backgrounds. And winter snows and holiday decorations make even the largest Victorian home cozy and inviting.

SPRING

A streetscape on Windham Street in early spring.

Left:
The green and red trim and snow-covered evergreens add to the holiday atmosphere of this charming Victorian cottage.

"Victoria House," one of the largest cottages in the camp meeting ground, is pretty in pink amid its awakening garden.

Dogwoods and azaleas
fill the front yard of this
South Windham home.

An old outhouse has been
turned into a charming garden
shed, but the half moon
symbol in the gable reveals its
former use.

A bed of phlox makes a spectacular summer display along the side of this white Queen Anne/Shingle style home. Note the variety of window sizes and shapes, including the arcade of round-arch windows and blinds, and the large stained-glass window.

Right:
Red potted and hanging flowers pop
against this crisp, white house on
Lewiston Avenue.

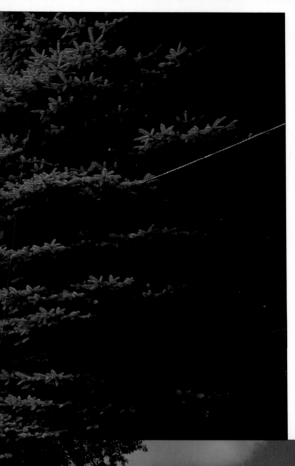

Bright red salvia play off
the cool greens of this
house on Windham Street.

This small Queen Anne is big on design features, including a tower and finial, striped awnings, and a variety of shingle patterns. Fall colors accentuate the red roof and accents.

AUTUMN

Pumpkins on the front steps send a cheerful welcome to visitors.

Left:
Window boxes overflow with annuals, and a flag for the Fourth of July.

Right:
A black metal Halloween witch and lantern are outlined against a neighbor's house on Windham Road.

106

A scarecrow in the garden and pumpkins under the balustrade are reminders of the harvest season.

WINTER

Geometric designs on the bargeboard and porch frieze contrast
with the circular holiday wreaths at the windows and doors.

Large garlands swoop along the front of the porch balustrade in a bold, but simple holiday statement.

Wreaths mix easily with folk art in this vernacular Italianate on Summit Street.